RABBIT STEW
FOR YOUR SOUL

20 RECIPES
with a dash of storytelling

by
BOB FORD

Mechanicsburg, PA USA

Published by Sunbury Press, Inc.
Mechanicsburg, Pennsylvania

www.sunburypress.com

Copyright © 2019 by Bob Ford.
Cover Copyright © 2019 by Sunbury Press, Inc.

Sunbury Press supports copyright. Copyright fuels creativity, encourages diverse voices, promotes free speech, and creates a vibrant culture. Thank you for buying an authorized edition of this book and for complying with copyright laws by not reproducing, scanning, or distributing any part of it in any form without permission. You are supporting writers and allowing Sunbury Press to continue to publish books for every reader. For information contact Sunbury Press, Inc., Subsidiary Rights Dept., PO Box 548, Mechanicsburg, PA 17007 USA or legal@sunburypress.com.

For information about special discounts for bulk purchases, please contact Sunbury Press Orders Dept. at (855) 338-8359 or orders@sunburypress.com.

To request one of our authors for speaking engagements or book signings, please contact Sunbury Press Publicity Dept. at publicity@sunburypress.com.

ISBN: 978-1-62006-711-6 (trade paperback)

Library of Congress Control Number:2019950734

FIRST SUNBURY PRESS EDITION: September 2019

Product of the United States of America
0 1 1 2 3 5 8 13 21 34 55

Designed by Alice Buchman
Photos by Bob Ford
Edited by Lawrence Knorr

Table of Contents

Introduction ... 3

Breakfast ... 5
- Bunny Breakfast Sandwich ... 6
- Hop Scotch Eggs ... 8
- SOS ... 10
- Two-Bunny Gravy ... 12

Lunch ... 15
- Buffalo Rabbit Wings ... 16
- Lagos Salad ... 18
- Mixed Game Bag Corn Soup ... 20
- Rabbit Stew ... 22
- Thumper Fajitas ... 24
- Wild Game Chili ... 26

Dinner ... 29
- Bunny Bratwurst ... 30
- Chicken Fried Rabbit ... 32
- Tourtière AKA Meat Pie ... 34
- Pasta with Meat Sauce ... 36
- Rabbit Cacciatore ... 38
- Rabbit in a Hole ... 40
- Rabbit Scampi ... 42
- Rabboli ... 44
- 40-Clove Rabbit ... 46
- Spicy Sauerkraut and Rabbit ... 48

Conclusion ... 50

Introduction

I have spent my entire life hunting, and rabbit hunting has been one of my passions since I was 13 years old. It is a sport that I enjoy because the hunt involves my beagles, who are both hunting partners and beloved pets. Yeah, I am one of those guys that have dogs on the couch and dog hair on my black pants. When you have hunted rabbits as long as I have, you end up eating a lot of rabbits.

Now, I have eaten a lot of fried rabbit. A lot of people have. It might be the single most common way to have wild rabbit, and I still eat it today. But I have spent decades finding new ways to eat rabbits. You find some of the results in this book, and it was hard to choose which recipes to include. I would, however, like to mention a few things.

First, I am a successful rabbit hunter. I am guessing that some readers will likewise be rabbit hunters. That being said, domesticated rabbits are very popular, I see them in grocery stores and farmers' markets regularly. Those domesticated species are larger, but the recipes still apply. Rabbit meat will increase in popularity with sustainable living being emphasized, and a trend of foodies and hunters cooperating has been a welcome development in recent years.

Secondly, I am a good home cook. I wrote the recipes with the presumption that the reader is also a good cook. I don't include instructions on how to make gravy, for instance. Naturally, you will alter ingredients for taste (don't use hot peppers if you don't like them). Wild rabbits can be a little tough, some can be a bit gamey in taste (especially hare shot in winter) and my intent is to focus on ways to enjoy the fruits of the field, maybe with a few recipes that are brand new to some. I have a few breakfast recipes, which would be a welcome addition to hunting camp.

Lastly, I am not a professional photographer. There are people who specialize in taking pictures of food. Some of the food you see in advertising has been painted or sprayed or altered in some other way that makes them "look" better than it actually looks. I took pictures of food that I was about to eat, the lighting wasn't perfect, and the camera was a cellphone. But they all taste good, and I hope that you enjoy trying a few of these recipes.

BREAKFAST

Bunny Breakfast Sandwich

Hop Scotch Eggs

SOS

Two-Bunny Gravy

Bunny Breakfast Sandwich

I went to Cape Cod to hunt rabbits with my friend Jason, and if you would have told me that I would see rabbits running along a beach, and stood by the seashore while I was hunting rabbits, I would have not believed it possible. But there we were, under a blue sky, the rabbits occasionally running along the beach, waves lapping at the feet of the dogs as they tried to continue the chase. The sunny day looked like it could have been summer, and the only reason you can tell from the pictures that it is not summer is that we are wearing long-sleeved shirts and hunting vests.

Any grocery store around me will offer chorizo, a popular Portuguese sausage. I had never heard of linguica before going to Cape Cod. If you ask the locals, they might even tell you that it is not a Portuguese sausage, but rather an Azorean specialty. The Azores are a string of islands off the coast of Portugal. Politically, they are part of Portugal. Culturally, I am told, the Azores are distinct. Anyway, on our first day of hunting, we pulled up to a local drive-through coffee shop.

"Want a breakfast sandwich?" Jason asked. The dogs were loaded into the dog box in his truck.

"Yeah, I will take one," I grabbed my wallet.

"I got it," Jason waved his hand to tell me to put my money away.

We crept closer to the speaker, where we would order.

"You want linguica?"

"What is that?" I asked. And then it was time to order.

"Two large coffees, and two linguica breakfast sandwiches," Jason decided for me.

"This is amazing," I said as we went down the road, eating my sandwich.

"I guess it isn't as common in other places," Jason said. I finished breakfast, drank my coffee, and we embarked upon my first ever hunt on a sandy beach.

"I usually sunburn at the beach," I said.

"Your face still might," Jason said, and he was right. It did. Great chases, great hound music, and we shot some rabbits. Back to his house for supper. It was fresh seafood from the Cape Cod waters—and linguica links.

"What is that?" I asked.

"Same thing we had for breakfast, but in links instead of patties. They were split lengthwise and cooked on a grill. The next morning, we went back to the local drive-through.

"Two large coffees and two linguica breakfast sandwiches," Jason said.

"Make that three," I said, "I think I can eat two."

"What the hell," he said, "Make that four sandwiches."

I grabbed my wallet, "My turn to pay."

I won't say that my linguica is as good, but these breakfast patties are tasty. I make them to remind me of rabbit hunting on the beach. There are ingredients I can't get (like piri piri peppers), and different makers of linguica have secrets. There is no complete list of seasonings on a package when you get it on the Cape. When Jason comes to visit, I always have him bring a few pounds of the real deal, but this breakfast sandwich is pretty darn good.

Ingredients: 1 rabbit, 1 pound of pork, garlic powder, sugar, salt, paprika, favorite cheese, eggs, and English muffins or croissant rolls.

1. I just buy a pork roast, typically, and cut it into one-pound pieces, removing any bone. I use one pound of pork for one rabbit, and two pounds for two rabbits. You get the picture. One rabbit is going to make 2 pounds of sausage when mixed with the pork. This is a good recipe for camp when you have lots of hungry people at breakfast. This recipe is for one rabbit, so adjust accordingly.
2. Debone a rabbit, add it to the one pound of pork that has been cubed. Run that all through your grinder and mix it up well.
3. Add 1 tablespoon each of garlic powder, sugar, salt, and paprika.
4. Add 1 teaspoon each of sugar, crushed red pepper, onion powder, and black pepper.
5. Mix it all thoroughly for an even distribution of spices. Make patties that fit your bread of choice. I like the larger, sandwich-sized English muffins, but I have used biscuits, croissant rolls, or even thick toast.
6. Cheese and egg are typical for a breakfast sandwich, but I have eaten these for supper on a hamburger bun with onions and mustard.

Hop Scotch Eggs

Do you remember getting milk delivered? So, do I, and it seems like a long time ago. Until recently. For the past couple years, we have been getting milk delivered once per week, from Vale Wood Farms. My wife, Renee, has a standing order: a half-gallon of milk, a pint of half and half for coffee, and a dozen eggs.

I leave in the morning with dogs, and I bring in the dairy before I leave. Now, it gets hard to know what will get used each week. When my stepson was still at home, a half-gallon of milk could disappear quickly if he was eating cereal. If he was not, then the milk would stack up. I started using milk in my coffee on those weeks since the half and half had a longer expiration date.

There were times when I would return home from the field, bring dogs into the house, and look in the fridge for some late breakfast/brunch. Sometimes there would be 3 dozen eggs looking at me. How in the world do I get rid of that many eggs? French Toast was my best guess. So, I would eat French toast to use up the eggs. The beagles would stare at me while I made French Toast. I won't lie, I hard-boiled a few eggs to give them when we had 3 dozen eggs monopolizing the refrigerator.

If I had an empty jar of banana peppers, I might put some hard-boiled eggs in the brine. You do it the way you would with pickled beets. The eggs have a yellow yolk, of course, but then also the whites turn a pastel yellow. They taste pretty good. One day, in the winter, I came home with one big rabbit. What would I do with one rabbit?

I butchered it, rinsed it, and put it in the crisper drawer, inside a sealed plastic container to soak. I saw the eggs. Dozens of them. Ever eat a Scotch egg? It is made with breakfast sausage. It gets molded around a soft-boiled egg (If they become hard-boiled by accident, I still eat them)) and fried. Often served with a spicy mustard sauce. I call mine a Hop Scotch egg. Rabbits hop. I can use seven eggs with one rabbit, and if you have eggs that need to be used, this is great.

Ingredients: 1 rabbit, 7 eggs, sage, thyme, sugar, rosemary, hot pepper flakes, bread crumbs or flour, vegetable oil, and mustard.

1. Soft-boil 4-5 eggs.
2. Debone and grind a rabbit.
3. Add 1 teaspoon each of sage, thyme, sugar.
4. ½ teaspoon of Rosemary, and ½ teaspoon of hot pepper flakes (optional).
5. Mix it all together well to distribute seasoning.
6. This is all rabbit, and as we know, rabbit is lean and will not pack Add two raw eggs and mix it well with your hands.
7. Take your peeled, soft-boiled eggs and put the meat around them, conforming to the shape of the eggs. 5 eggs are nice, 4 will have a thicker layer of sausage.
8. Roll the finished product in some bread crumbs or flour. I prefer bread crumbs, but sometimes we are out of them. The raw egg whisked into the meat earlier will make either crumbs or flour adhere nicely.
9. Use a deep skillet with vegetable oil, and roll the eggs until the meat is thoroughly cooked.
10. Serve with your favorite mustard. Or whatever dipping sauce you like. Or, quite honestly, they are good without any dunking.

SOS

There is a restaurant near some of my hunting spots called Green Acres. There is a sign on the door that says "No Credit Cards" and one on the cash register which reads "No checks" so you pretty much know that you better have cash when you go in there. I am not one to hunt on a full stomach, so I tend to just have coffee and maybe a piece of toast before I get into the woods.

After a morning hunt, I like to pop into Green Acres. It is the kind of place that serves breakfast all day, but it isn't a chain. Oh, and they make the most rocking hot pepper relish that you have had. It comes to you in a mason jar. It is made right there on the premises, and that stuff goes perfectly with the home fries.

My wife, Renee, makes fun of me because I always carry some cash. One time, we were traveling, and she wanted to stop at a fast-food place. I forget what it was, I think a McDonald's.

"No can do," I told her.

"Why not?" Renee asked, "It will be fast."

"You took my cash from my wallet, and I have not replaced it yet."

"You don't need cash."

"At a drive-through? Yeah, you do."

"Have you been to one in the last decade?"

"I think so."

"Evidently not, they take cards now," she sighed. She was right.

One Saturday, a few years ago, she was in a mood for breakfast. It was late morning, and we were returning from a meeting.

"Where can we get a good breakfast?" she asked, knowing that I travel the area we were in more than she does.

"My favorite spot is a few miles away," I said.

"Good," she said, "I will buy."

"Okay," I snickered.

"What are you laughing at?" she slapped me, "Why do you think I always try to get out of paying?"

"Sorry," I said, and took her inside. She read the sign explaining that credit cards won't work.

"I am local enough to write a check, right?"

"I think so," I said. We ate. I got the chipped beef over toast, commonly called SOS. I usually get it when I am done rabbit hunting, about 11 o'clock in the morning. The small is two pieces of toast, the large is 4. Four pieces of toast, with the chipped beef gravy, and the coffee that just keeps getting topped off will make you very full. Especially if you get the hot relish with home fries too. We walked up to the register to leave. "You said that my check was local enough to work?" Renee said in panic, seeing the sign that forbids checks.

"It is local enough."

"The sign says no checks!"

"Oh," I said, "I know. Make that check out to me." I grabbed my wallet to pay.

"What kinda place doesn't take checks or cards?" she asked.

"A place with really good food," I said.

"That is true. It was great. You think you are so smart! Let's see you make that SOS out of rabbit!" Challenge accepted.

SOS is made with a dried, often smoked beef. It then soaks up all the goodness of that white gravy.

Ingredients: 1-2 rabbits, your favorite bread, and ingredients for your favorite country gravy recipe.

1. I cook 1-2 rabbits in one of those fancy new pressure cookers. 30 minutes takes the meat from raw to falling off the bone. You can also use a slow cooker until the meat is falling off the bone. Next, I will smoke it.
2. The reason for cooking it first is to ensure that the temperature gets hot enough to kill tularemia. I want to smoke the meat, not cook to a crisp.
3. This is a breakfast recipe, but you can eat it any time of day. I usually make this meat the night before. It seems a waste to use all that charcoal and wood chips for the 15 minutes of smoke time. So, I have a cookout for supper, making whatever I want, and then I still have all those hot coals. Soak the woodchips in water while you are cooking supper. I like applewood, but hickory is nice. Use whatever food-grade wood you have or whatever your store sells if you are buying it.
4. Pick all the meat off the bones.
5. Pile the meat on some aluminum foil, and make it into a pouch that is open on the top. Season with salt and pepper to taste.
6. Put those woodchips on your charcoal grill. The meat is already cooked, so I spread the coals to the outside perimeter. I place the meat in the center, with no direct heat. Those woodchips go on top of the charcoal, and I put the lid on top of the grill, closing the vent most of the way, and give the meat 15 minutes. It will get smokier the longer you leave it in there. I find 15 minutes to be plenty.
7. Put the meat in the refrigerator for the night, and the next morning make your favorite white gravy/flour gravy/country gravy or whatever you call it. My French-Canadian mother-in-law calls it béchamel. Add the rabbit.
8. You can go all out and make homemade bread. I like the potato bread that is prominent here in Pennsylvania, I just buy it pre-sliced in the grocery store.

Two-Bunny Gravy

I have been married long enough to get in trouble. I forget things. Especially in rabbit season. I tend to hunt the last hour of daylight almost every day of the rabbit season. I work during the morning and the afternoon, and I almost always have a Bible Study or meeting in the evening. So, I just hunt the last hour of daylight. Okay, sometimes the last hour and a half.

My wife, Renee, knows that I do this, and we never eat an early supper because she knows that I will be out. Sometimes, however, I am given orders to get home early. One day, after a particularly great last hour of daylight, I got back on the road and headed for home. As soon as I got into cell phone range my phone started bleeping and beeping like R2D2. I glanced down and saw that I had missed many phone calls from my wife and that she had left a lot of texts. I decided to give her a call. I hate texting while sitting in my kitchen, let alone try it at a stop sign. I have been nearly wrecked numerous times by people looking at their phones while driving, and they veer into my lane. "Hey, buddy! You get half the road, but it ain't the middle half!" My buddy Lee always says when we are driving and someone decides to text their way into our lane.

I don't even hold the phone to my ear. That distracts me. So, I use the speakerphone and hold the thing like a CB radio.

"Where have you been?" Renee answered the phone.

"Honey, I wa-"

"Hunting. You were hunting. I saw that Duke and Diamond were not in the house," she yelled.

"I do that all the time honey, why did you ask?"

"Because," she said, "We talked this morning, and I told you that I made plans to meet some friends for supper."

"Really?" I asked

"Yeah. We talked about it for like 20 minutes."

"You were talking about how tough it was at work, and how stressed out your friend is right now."

"Yes," she sighed "And then I told you that we were meeting her and her husband for supper."

"I am sorry," I said. I tuned her out when she began talking about work stuff. She is on the computer all day, and I do almost nothing on a computer other than word processing.

"Will you turn off that speakerphone!"

The speakerphone drives her crazy. Really crazy. I turned it off and put the phone to my ear.

"Want me to meet you wherever you are eating?"

"It depends," she said, "Are you wearing hunting bibs that are filthy and splattered with rabbit blood?"

"Yep."

"No, just go home and change. I have a pie in the fridge, I will suggest that they come to the house to meet you and we can have dessert and coffee." And we did.

That wasn't the worst mistake in the whole world, but it takes a few days for all the tension to fade. Now, my wife loves mashed potatoes, so I made her some with sausage gravy. I even followed a trick that one of my parishioners taught me—put a thick slice of Velveeta cheese into the potatoes along with the butter before whipping them. It was a trick to get the kids to eat them. My 2-bunny gravy has two options—you can put it over biscuits for breakfast, or over whipped potatoes for supper.

Ingredients: 2 rabbits, brown sugar, sage, nutmeg, allspice, marjoram, and your favorite country gravy recipe.

1. Two deboned rabbits, coarse ground.
2. 1 tablespoon each of brown sugar, sage, and pepper.
3. ½ teaspoon each of nutmeg, allspice, and marjoram.
4. Mix all the seasonings into the meat.
5. Cook the meat and when it is browned, add it to your favorite country gravy/flour gravy. I cook the meat in butter or oil since there is no fat like there is with pork sausage.
6. Serve over biscuits for breakfast.
7. If I am making this gravy for supper, in a separate pan I will dice up an onion as small as I can get it. Sauté it until soft and golden, then add 1-3 cloves of finely chopped garlic to the onions and cook the garlic is golden. I add the onions and garlic to the sausage gravy at the very end and serve over potatoes or rice.

LUNCH

Buffalo Rabbit Wings

Lagos Salad

Mixed Game Bag Corn Soup

Rabbit Stew

Thumper Fajitas

Wild Game Chili

Buffalo Rabbit Wings

When it comes to chicken, there is no part of the bird more expensive than the wings. At one time, this was not the case. It was not until Buffalo wings emerged in the city of Buffalo that the wings became a highly sought-after commodity. And even then, it took a little while to catch on in all places. When I was a kid, my mom would go to a butcher shop, and if she was regularly buying meat there, she would be given the wings for free, to make soup. It wasn't even considered a loss. The rest of the chicken was considered the valuable portion, and the tiny amount of meat on the wings was negligible—the store absorbed the cost to keep loyal customers.

I am always surprised at the cost of chicken wings in restaurants. Over $1 per wing, most of the time. That just seems crazy to me. The way that I fell into this recipe was by soaking rabbits in water overnight, as I always do. I like to soak them one to three days to get rid of the blood and make it easier to remove the tiny bits of lead from where the rabbit was shot. As we all know, you can't get it all, but you can work hard to keep the rabbit rich in iron and not lead.

I had a few rabbits soaking in a big plastic container, ready to snap the lid shut, when my wife, Renee, yelled to me, "Hurry up, we are going to be late! We are meeting friends for wing night. I don't know why you had to hunt until dark on a Friday!" As Renee yelled at me about chicken wings, I was just about to snap the lid shut on the Tupperware container to give the meat a soak overnight. Some of the front legs were floating at the top, and I thought to myself, "Those kinda look like chicken wings!"

That evening, as people took advantage of the wing special, I decided that there must be a way to make the front legs of a rabbit into wings. After a few attempts, I decided that the best method was to bread the legs, and fry the outside, to give a texture akin to the skin that is on chicken. But to get the wings tender, I found that they had to bake in the oven at a relatively low temperature. It worked best to keep them covered in the sauce, so they did not dry. This is one of my favorite recipes, and I routinely save all the front legs, freezing them in isolation from the rest of the rabbit meat until I get a bunch of "wings" to cook.

One year, when the Steelers made the Super Bowl, Renee decided to host a Super Bowl party. I cooked a bunch of these rabbit wings, with various hot sauces. I went to a local chicken wing specialty restaurant, Quaker Steak and Lube, and bought their sauces to use with the rabbit wings. One of the guests at our party was a gal that works with Renee, and she had no idea that she wasn't eating chicken wings until someone asked me why the wings were shaped a little funny!

Ingredients: Front legs from 6-8 rabbits, egg wash, bread crumbs, and your favorite hot wing sauce.

1. Save up the front legs from your rabbit hunts in a gallon bag in the freezer.
2. Dredge the "wings" in egg and bread crumbs.
3. Fry the front legs (wings) in a pan for just a minute or two.
4. Place the front legs of the rabbits in an oven-safe pan or casserole dish.
5. Cover them in your favorite hot sauce.
6. Bake at 300 for 3 hours—nice and tender.

Lagos Salad

Lagos is Greek for hare or rabbit. In the summer, when it is hot, I love a chilled salad, with some chicken on top. Or rabbit. As long as I have owned beagles, it has been difficult to garden. Gardens attract rabbits, and it is not at all uncommon for my dogs to go into the yard for a bathroom break and find a rabbit either inside the dog fence, or sitting just outside, near the vegetable garden. Chaos, of course, ensues. The noise is intense, and the hounds will throw themselves against the chain-link fence and try to tunnel under it. As a result, much of my fence is lined with a moat of cement. They dig, I fill it in.

The rabbit problem can sometimes lead to a jailbreak, and the next thing I know, I am running around my town of fewer than 500 people, trying to catch beagles that have put the chubby town rabbit on the most rigorous exercise plan of its life. If you had told me, when I installed the fence, that a full-grown rabbit could fit through one diamond of chain link, I would not have believed it. Oh, trust me, they can fit through one square, on a dead run, and barely slow down. The dogs, on a sprint and chasing with their eyes rather than their noses, will inevitably bounce off the fence. Then they start trying to find a way through, over, or under.

Of course, the dogs are often extra amped in the summer, because when the temperatures soar and the humidity rises, I often do not take them afield to chase bunnies, for concern of heat stroke or other problems. I will run them on rainy days, and very early in the morning. In other words, they are not as tired as they typically might be when the weather is cooler and they run a dozen miles per day. So, when I open the door of the house in the summer to let them go into the fenced yard, they charge out there, looking for some poor rabbit munching clover, unaware that it will have to run, and fast! The garden attracts the rabbits, but it also contains the ingredients for lagos salad.

Ingredients: 1 rabbit, 1 large onion, cherry tomatoes, feta cheese, a bell pepper, a cucumber, capers and stuffed grape leaves (from the supermarket), and your favorite salad dressing.

1. Whatever greens you grow, or buy. I like spinach and leaf lettuce.
2. Cut up a big onion.
3. Add some cherry or grape tomatoes.
4. Feta cheese is customary, but I have used fresh Mozzarella too.
5. A bell pepper cut up into small pieces. I like a yellow or orange one, but green is popular too.
6. Chop up a cucumber. I like to cut long strips, and not use center seeds. Then dice the strips.
7. Add the other store-bought stuff: Dolmades (stuffed grape leaves), olives, and capers.
8. Put that bowl in the refrigerator to get nice and cold.
9. Parboil a quartered rabbit for 20 minutes, then coat it with a batter of your choice. I have used anything from buttermilk to Bisquick out of the box. Fry the rabbit, and when it is done pull the salad out of the fridge and add the protein.
10. A Greek dressing is traditional, but I have used Italian, Caesar, or even 1,000 Island.

Mixed Game Bag Corn Soup

One autumn day, my wife, Renee was fighting a cold. Or the flu. Or bronchitis. Or something. A "virus" is what they typically tell her, and then she comes home to bark and cough and be miserable. One thing about house dogs, they can tell when you are not feeling well. Sad? Sick? Sore? Any one of those sentiments will result in a lap full of beagles at my house.

"Is there anything I can do for you?" I asked Renee. Her hair was beyond disheveled as she lay motionless on the couch, face down in a pillow. A beagle was on her back, another between her legs, and a third on her pillow, wedged between her head and the arm of the couch.

"Reth theeeve rog offuv vee," She said.

"What?"

She picked her face up from the pillow, "Get these dogs off of me."

"Okay," I nodded my head. Now, she did not specify how I should do that. So, I loaded them into the truck and went hunting. Before I left, I put a glass of ginger ale on the table to get stale—she likes it that way when she is sick, and I also made sure to put the remote control for the television beside her on the stool. You know those little wooden stools they sell for a kitchen bar? We don't have a kitchen bar, but we use those for food trays. I sped away, giving her a break from the dogs, and me a break from the coughing. The hunting was good. Well, the rabbit chasing was good.

The cover was so dense that I had trouble getting a shot at a rabbit. But, a couple of doves were flushed by the dogs as they pushed the rabbit past me. I got both. A woodcock also burst out of the marsh, and it fell. Granted, I missed three other woodcocks before that. The chase continued, and I managed to see the rabbit. And miss. A large fox squirrel presented itself, as it ran up a tree and sent a vocal disdain at the dogs below. The game vest was getting pretty diverse now. Finally, I shot the rabbit they were chasing. My cell phone rang, as I kept it close in case Renee called. "Hello," I said.

"Thanks for the flat ginger ale," Renee said.

"No problem."

"Can you get me some cold medicine? I am so stuffy."

"On the way." I loaded the dogs and went to the grocery store, heading straight to the pharmaceutical section to get cold medicine. Then, I wondered what to do with a squirrel, a woodcock, 2 doves, and a rabbit. It sounded like a deranged 4 days of Christmas. I started thinking about how my mom always made chicken soup when someone was sick, but how I always liked it a better a few days later when it turned into chicken corn soup. I had doves and woodcock, not chicken. Plus, a rabbit and a squirrel. That was my first time cooking mixed game bag corn soup. I often make it when I have managed to shoot a few birds. Grouse, pheasant, doves, squirrels, and rabbits have all made this recipe, in various proportions and combinations.

Ingredients: Birds and rabbits from a successful hunt, chicken stock or broth, 4 cans of creamed corn, 1-2 cups of finely diced carrots, 1 can of French onion soup, black pepper, garlic powder, basil, oregano, Old Bay, and 1-2 bags of egg noodles.

1. Boil meat off the bone from birds, squirrels, and bunnies and put the meat in the BIG pot.
2. Add broth or stock to the pot.
3. Add a can of store-bought French onion soup.
4. Add 4 cans of creamed corn.
5. Cut up a half bag of carrots really small.
6. Add a big dusting (tablespoon plus a bit more) of each: black pepper, garlic powder, basil, oregano, Old Bay.
7. Let that all simmer for a few hours, add water if necessary.
8. Add big bag of frozen corn and 2 bags of egg noodles—let boil 10 minutes.
9. Melt in butter and a large shake of Parmesan cheese at the end.

Rabbit Stew

Perhaps no other rabbit recipe of mine has been better received than my rabbit stew. Years ago, I took a big batch of it to a tailgate at Heinz stadium to watch the Steelers host the Cleveland Browns. A friend of mine had tickets given to him, and we decided to hang out in the parking lot and see all the semi-organized chaos that goes along with a Steelers tailgate. It was cold outside. The kind of cold that prompted me to wear my best cold weather hunting gear, including the boots that will make my feet sweat to walk any distance.

We cooked sausages with onions. We had some sides that we brought as well. Then, we heated the rabbit stew that I had cooked the night before and refrigerated. People started flocking to us. Including a reporter from the local KDKA channel in Pittsburgh. KDKA, of course started as a radio station, and some claim it is the first commercial station in the United States. The reporter talked to us, as she was making her rounds to assess the tailgating food at the stadium parking lots. She was intrigued by the smell of the food and was hesitant to try it. After all, it was wild game. But, there is a camera on the whole conversation, and after being urged to try the stew, she did and looked at the camera to say that it was really good.

The tailgaters next to us were people that traveled from Ohio to cheer for Cleveland. They all sampled the stew, which by now was being doled out in Styrofoam cups and the whole 6 quarts was going fast. One Browns fan was a little tipsy, and she wanted a second cup to get warm. "Can I get some more bunny soup?" she said.

"Sure," I replied.

"I'll do anything you ask," she said.

"You don't have to do anything," I replied.

"We can go in my van."

"Nah, but you can have the stew."

"Is it because you are married, cause I don't care."

"Well," I said, "My supervisor could fire me."

"Who is that?"

"The bishop. And my boss could send me to hell," I continued.

"What?" she asked.

"Jesus is my boss. He could send me to hell. And after being fired and sent to hell, I really shudder to think what my wife might do."

Ingredients: 5 rabbits, 5-7 strips of bacon, 1 large onion, bag of baby carrots, tomato paste, 5-7 potatoes, large bag of spinach, black pepper, rosemary, celery seed, crushed red pepper, chicken stock, and basil.

1. Cook 5-7 pieces of bacon in skillet until crisp, then break it up into your pot.
2. Caramelize an onion. mushrooms (I like wild oysters) and garlic in the bacon grease. Then put it in the pot.
3. De-bone 5 rabbits and add it.
4. Cube 5 -7 spuds ... I like the yellow ones. Sometimes I will add a bag of corn and an extra rabbit instead of putting potatoes in the stew. If so, I serve it over home fried potatoes.
5. Throw in a bag of carrots cut up small.
6. Add 8 ounces or so of tomato paste.
7. Add a big batch of spinach—it shrinks.
8. Add lots of fresh ground black pepper, basil and rosemary to taste, a little bit of crushed red pepper if you like it, a few shakes of old bay seasoning, a dash of celery flakes.
9. Cover all in chicken stock.
10. Cook until tender—several hours on simmer should do. Stir, and don't let it stick to the pot. I prefer to leave it in a slow cooker all day while I am at work.

Thumper Fajitas

Fajitas are one of the things that I will often make. Like, every week. I am still baffled as to how a fully-cooked rotisserie chicken from a grocery store will cost less money than a raw chicken of the same size. When we get done with supper, I strip the bird of all remaining meat and save it for fajitas the next day. In fact, any leftover meat can find its way into a tortilla shell at my house. Roast beef, pork loin, venison roast, or whatever.

I like to remove the tender meat from the back of rabbits the same way that I remove the back straps from a deer. Of course, the back straps from a rabbit are much smaller. However, like the venison counterpart, they are very tender and boneless. When I butcher rabbits, I keep all the back straps, or loin, separated, freezing them each day until I have a bunch.

"I will bring lunch tomorrow," I said to Andy, a hunting partner of mine.

"What are you making?"

"It is a surprise."

"Yeah, well, it better be good, or we are going to Subway."

"Dude, trust me, it is gonna be better than Subway!"

The next day, Andy and I met at a favorite hunting spot to put the dogs onto some fresh snow and run the bunnies. My Rebel dog was a beast on fresh snow because he used his eyes to look for rabbit tracks in the snow. You would think that all dogs would learn this trick, but they do not. Andy had a couple of dogs that did the same, and we were off to the races. There is just something about the good hound music on fresh snow that makes my soul smile. You can see the rabbits better too, and where they may sneak past you in the autumn goldenrod, they are much less elusive on fresh snow. We shot a few rabbits within a couple hours and relocated to another spot.

"You got three already?" Andy asked.

"Yeah."

"You're too eager."

"I am letting some go too," I said, "I want you to shoot some."

"I am just happy to hear the dogs," Andy said, "I got one today."

Now, what Andy meant by "too eager" was that I left the dirt road., and I did not stand at the edge of the field. Andy was no fan of getting into the thick stuff. Very often, a rabbit will stay inside the cover, right at the edge, and never emerge where you can see it from a dirt path or a mowed field. I tend to step just into the cover and look for a spot with some visibility, even if it is only for 10 or 15 yards.

At the second spot, I had the dogs pass and the rabbit must have known I was there, it ran where I could not see it. The dogs were pressuring hard, and I heard Andy fire twice.

"Get it?" I yelled

"Yep!" he called back.

Soon another rabbit was up and moving. It took over an hour to even see this one. Eventually, it got far in front of the dogs after doubling back on its own tracks and making the scent difficult. It hopped right up to me and stood still. It turned its head around to look towards the baying sound of the beagles. That was my fourth rabbit for the day and a limit. I put my gun away and just handled dogs.

"It's all you," I said.

"Let's go," Andy grabbed his gun and headed into a field with round bales of hay. I took the dogs into the pines. The rabbit ran and ran, but never came out into the field.

"Most rabbits aren't suicidal," I said, "You may have to get in the brush."

"I am thinning the stupid rabbits from the local population," Andy said, "If it comes out here, I will get it. I am happy. Let's listen."

It did cross the field, eventually, but too far away to shoot. As it got late, we picked up the dogs.

"What are we eating?" Andy asked.

"You'll see," I fired up the propane stove.

"Wait a minute," he said, "I am hungry now. How long is this gonna take?"

"Not long." I had cooked the peppers, onion, and garlic the night before. It was in the cooler with the salsa and guacamole. I put the cooked veggies in a pan with the raw back straps that I thawed. I added a little vegetable oil. When the meat was almost done, I put the tortillas in a separate pan. They were stacked up in aluminum foil covering, and I kept flipping the whole lot of them to heat them. Then we ate. While still eating, Andy threw his two rabbits into my truck.

"What are you doing?" I asked.

"That was delicious. You need to make those again." A sad look came over his face.

"Why are you so upset?" I gave him another warmed tortilla.

"I am just wishing that I would have got more serious about killing rabbits. I would have two more to give you for the next fajitas!"

I do this dish with back straps, fried. But you can also cook the meat off the hind legs in a slow cooker, remove the bones, and throw that meat into the onions and peppers. I think of my departed friend, Andy, every time I cook them.

Ingredients: The backs of 5-6 rabbits, onion, favorite peppers, garlic cloves, tortillas, salsa, guacamole, shredded cheese, and hot sauce.

1. Save a bunch of the "back straps" from rabbits.
2. Cook an onion and peppers until soft.
3. Cook the strips of rabbit loin with the peppers and onion.
4. I like to add a smashed clove of garlic (or two) at the end.
5. Microwave tortillas for 30 secs in a wrapped towel to soften them.
6. I like to have some cheese, guacamole, salsa, and hot sauce to add to the top.
7. When I cook thin cut venison steak as well as rabbit I call this dish Bambi & Thumper fajitas.

Wild Game Chili

One of my favorite things to eat in the winter is chili. I like to let it cook all day, and I like to make enough that there are leftovers. There is a lot of argument around chili. I've heard people say that there is no room for beans in chili. Beans are flat out wrong, in some parts of the country. Heck, I was in an airport talking to a guy from Texas, and he told me that he wasn't even a fan of any sort of tomatoes being present in his chili.

This is all to say that I do not really consider myself a chili expert. Heck, I am from Pennsylvania. In my own house, there are debates about how many peppers and what kinds of peppers (chilis) can go into the chili. Beans are a part of chili up here, for bad or steam rolling good, and when my wife makes chili I have trouble distinguishing it from the premixed sloppy joe packs that you can buy in the grocery store. Her chili tastes just like sloppy joes, but with kidney beans added.

If I make a big pot of chili the way I like it, it will be too hot for my wife to eat. Hungarian Wax is about as hot as she can handle. I can always tell if the batch of peppers that I chose is too hot for her because she will only eat one bowl, and use heavily buttered bread and a glass of milk to go with it. Then, it is almost assured that the rest of the chili will have to be eaten by me alone. Sometimes I have to freeze it in quart portions. These will find their way into my lunch as the hunting season progresses, and is a favorite meal after a morning hunt. I love to sit in the truck, steam rolling from the thermos, the scent of chili filling the cab. Sometimes I will eat it every day for a week until it is gone. If you asked me to name one food that gets better from reheating it, I would say chili.

If I am baffled that my wife won't eat peppers, I know that I confuse her with crackers. I love a bowl of chili with almost an entire sleeve of saltine crackers. Yeah, I know that this is also considered chili blasphemy in certain parts of the country. I also like chili with those oyster crackers piled into the bottom of the bowl. I have used Ritz crackers and even those Chicken in a Biskit crackers that come in a box. That is pretty good.

The widow of a retired pastor in my parish taught me a good trick too. I can't believe that I never thought of it. She gets Frito corn chips to add to her chili. I know, I am amazed that I did not discover that trick either. I tend to have good deer seasons so I like to mix my rabbit meat with some venison. It is a good use of the ground venison, as it is too lean to pack into a burger, just like rabbit. But hey, I have also been known to make a batch with just rabbit meat. It is perfect for a winter day with a snowstorm barreling down on us off the Great Lakes or a pounding nor'easter piling up feet at the door.

I like this recipe with hare because I find hare to have a gamier taste—they sort of taste like the evergreens where I find them. I think they stand up to spicy recipes really well.

Ingredients: 2-4 rabbits, 2 pounds of venison, Onion, banana peppers, hot peppers, garlic cloves tomato sauce, tomato paste, black pepper, paprika, cumin, oregano, and a can of kidney beans.

1. Grind up the meat of 3 or 4 hare (or rabbits). Mix this with an equal amount of ground venison and fry it with the following vegetables cut really fine: an onion, 5-6 banana peppers, 5-6 hot peppers (your choice), and 2 garlic cloves.
2. Put the cooked meat (and the peppers, onion, and garlic) in a crockpot.
3. Add a jar of tomato sauce and a small can of tomato paste.
4. Add the beans that you typically use for chili. I only use kidney beans, but lots of folks use other kinds.
5. Add a pinch each of the following spices: black pepper, paprika, cumin, oregano.
6. Add a little water if it needs it, or beer to follow the recipe the way I learned it.
7. Go hunting for the day and return to supper.

DINNER

Bunny Bratwurst

Chicken Fried Rabbit

Tourtière AKA Meat Pie

Pasta with Meat Sauce

Rabbit Cacciatore

Rabbit in a Hole

Rabbit Scampi

Rabboli

40-Clove Rabbit

Spicy Sauerkraut and Rabbit

Bunny Bratwurst

I grew up in a neighborhood that was primarily German-American, and sauerkraut was a staple. My dad made sauerkraut in crocks and we would freeze it and can it. We ate it all winter, and in fact, by the end of the following summer we often still had some left from the previous year. So, as we got ready to make new sauerkraut, we would give away the leftovers from the previous batch. There was no shortage of takers, and it was popular at family cookouts. I still say that there is no other way to eat a hotdog than with sauerkraut, mustard, and raw onion. Not only would he make sauerkraut from the cabbage we grew in the garden, but he would also buy cabbage when it was on sale to make more.

As a kid, I didn't really like the taste, but there was no way around eating it. So, parents started by cooking the hotdogs in sauerkraut. You got a little taste of the stuff that way. You would put the hotdog on the bun, add mustard or ketchup, and when you bit into the frankfurter, you got some sauerkraut taste in the juices. Next, they would bury a few strands of kraut in your mashed potatoes. Before you knew it, you would be voluntarily eating the fermented cabbage and going back for seconds. Dad always cooked pork with his sauerkraut, and he preferred to eat it in the winter. He was not a fan of mom cooking a pork roast with sauerkraut during the summer. The house got way too hot.

One year, the factory was on strike and it lasted most of the summer. It went on long enough, that all the employees qualified for food stamps. Dad wouldn't take them. He was a proud man, and he worked constantly. He used his vacation time to do carpenter work for people and made a better wage those weeks than he would have earned at work. Whenever someone took vacation or got sick, he volunteered for overtime. He worked more eighty-hour weeks than he did forty-hour weeks.

"It seems odd," I once said to Andy Purnell, "You and I hang out and train beagles all the time. Like we are right now. I never thought about it as a kid, but I do not think my dad had any friends. I mean, he got along with people, but he never went places with them. He was either at work or at home."

"Everybody has a best friend," Andy said. "Did he get phone calls?"

"Yeah."

"Well," Andy said, "Whoever called him the most was his best friend."

"Hmm."

"What?" Andy said, "Can you remember who called the most?"

"Yep," I nodded my head.

"Who was it?"

"Overtime."

As the strike went on, dad had to use the food stamps, but he was embarrassed and told my mom to drive to a grocery store almost an hour away from home. We ate a lot of sauerkraut that summer, and there was none left to give away in the fall. Hotdogs and bratwurst cooked in sauerkraut and served over mashed potatoes. We ate that a lot. I was thinking about that summer when I invented my bunny bratwurst recipe.

Note: I fast-cook the bratwurst, meaning I make the sausage and cook it immediately, so there is no curing salt listed here in the ingredients.

Ingredients: 3 rabbits, 2 pounds of bacon, sausage casings, garlic powder, mustard powder, onion powder, paprika, black pepper, sage, and ranch dressing mix (the powder).

1. Debone 2 1/2 lbs. of rabbit or hare.
2. Grind 2 lbs. of the cheapest bacon you can find with the rabbit meat.
3. You could use fatback instead of bacon, but the bacon adds a unique taste.
4. Add 2 tablespoons each of garlic, mustard powder, paprika, garlic powder, onion powder.
5. Add one tablespoon each of black pepper, sage, & dry Ranch dressing mix (it was an experiment).
6. Add 1/3 cup of salt.
7. Mix well and put into casings. I use a KitchenAid, but you may have a sausage grinder.
8. When the bratwurst are in the casings, I brown them and then add to the sauerkraut to finish Sometimes I cook the bratwurst entirely in the sauerkraut and do not brown first.
9. I start cooking sauerkraut the day before I make the bratwurst. I add a chopped onion to the sauerkraut at the start and cook them together to sweeten it a bit.

Chicken Fried Rabbit

We live close to a Cracker Barrel restaurant. In fact, there are a few that aren't all that far away. We never go to them. When we are traveling, however, my wife loves to go there.

"Why do you always want to stop here?" I asked my wife, Renee, as we pulled into a Cracker Barrel near Binghamton, New York. The traffic is a nightmare there, but we always stop.

"Because I like it!"

"You like Binghamton?"

"No, I like Cracker Barrel."

"Then why do we never go to the one close to home?"

"I like Cracker Barrel while we are traveling. It isn't fast food, but you know what you are getting, and you can relax from all the driving."

The waitress gave us menus. I didn't need it. I always get the same thing, the country fried steak. Or chicken fried, as I called it as a kid. In fact, it is the only time I ever eat the stuff. We were on our way up north to attend a dog competition and had been on the road for a few hours. We ordered our food, and she ran into the gift shop to see what she might want to get after we were done eating. She always browses the store while the food is cooking. After eating, we continued our trip and arrived at the beagle club where we camped for a couple of days, and enjoyed the competition. Beagle clubs serve meals and they are affordable, filling, and good. But after a few days in the woods, we headed for home and my wife was looking for a sit-down meal.

"It's almost noon. Want to stop for food?" I asked Renee.

"Not yet," she said. I looked at the mile marker and the clock. We would be in Binghamton in an hour and a half. Sure enough, as we neared I-81, she spoke, "Want another country fried steak?"

"Okay," I said, knowing that it was inevitable.

Later that year, in the fall, I was hunting rabbits in the early part of November and the weeds, brush, and briars were thick and high. After a lot of rabbit chasing, I finally saw the rabbit, but it was running away from me by the time I spotted it. This happened a few more times until finally, I saw the rabbit before it saw me. It went into the game vest. The dogs ran two more rabbits, and I never did see them, not even once. They snuck past me in the thick cover.

On the way home, I was trying to figure out what to cook with just one rabbit. I passed a billboard advertising the Cracker Barrel close to our house, and I started thinking of a great idea…

You need that meat tenderizing, cube-shaped, mallet thing with the little spikes that mostly gets used for bashing bags of ice.

Ingredients: 1 rabbit per person, seasoned flour, buttermilk, and egg wash.

1. Remove the meat from the bones of a rabbit. One rabbit makes one steak.
2. Use the tenderizing mallet to flatten the boneless meat, while meshing it together into one larger piece that resembles a steak in shape. It may hold together very loosely. Pound it between two pieces of wax paper to keep your kitchen tidy. It will splatter otherwise.
3. Season your flour to taste. I use Old Bay, black pepper, garlic powder, onion powder, and paprika. A teaspoon of each.
4. Take the "steak" and dredge it in egg & buttermilk, then the seasoned flour, then the egg & buttermilk mixture, and lastly the flour again. You may have to be careful to keep the steak in one piece.
5. Fry the rabbit steaks in vegetable oil. Do not flip the steak until it has cooked long enough to brown and keep its shape. It will crumble if you flip too soon.
6. Make your gravy—everybody has their own recipe.

Tourtière AKA Meat Pie

"I want to make a tourtiere for Christmas Eve," my wife, Renee said to me.

"Oh yeah?" I said, "What is that?"

"It is pie, made with ground meat. Usually pork and beef."

"Oh," I said, "A meat pie."

"Well, there is more to it than that."

"Sure," I said, "Can we use rabbit?"

"I suppose," she shrugged, but the key is to have more than one meat.

"That doe that I killed in deer season was tough and old. We made a lot of ground meat from that deer."

"Hmm," Renee began plotting, "I think we may be onto something here."

Renee is from the part of New York that borders Quebec. Her mom was born in the United States, but her maternal grandparents only spoke French. Her mom only started speaking English when she went to school. My mother-in-law, Jeanine, still breaks into French-Canadian when she is upset. She is constantly cussing me out in French.

Jeanine now lives here in Pennsylvania where we can be close to her in her golden years, but when she still lived on the northern border, we would go see her every year around Christmas time. She lived in a small house with a bunch of cats (I am allergic to cats) and she kept the thermostat at what felt like 90 degrees in the winter. When we went to visit, we would get a hotel room, and we picked one that allowed dogs. I always took one dog with me—Rebel. Rebel could behave in any situation and was the most misnamed dog I have ever owned. He was perfectly obedient. My wife got permission for me to hunt snowshoe hare on a farm located close to where her mother lived.

"You got hare here?" I said to the farmer, looking at the three-foot-deep snow, and grabbing my snowshoes so that I could walk.

"You put dat der dog in da cedar trees," he answered in his north country accent, "And der will be so many tracks he won't know which way ta go."

"Thank you!"

He was right, and I quickly discovered that the fee for a nonresident of New York to hunt small game was well worth it. We were in town for a week, and my standard practice was to get out and hunt during the day, and then we would go out for supper and visit with my in-laws and Renee's old friends from high school and college. It was Christmas time, so even her relatives and friends that had moved away were home visiting, and Renee got to catch up with all of them.

On the fourth day of hunting, I saw the farmer again. "Getting any?" he asked me.

"Oh yeah," I said, "Especially once I crossed that old railroad bed. Lots of them in those cedars."

"Oh yeah?" he said, "What railroad bed?"

"It is in there a mile or so."

"You walk that far on da snowshoes?" he asked.

"Yeah. Well, the dog followed the hare there."

"I see," he said, "You was in Canada. No big deal before September 11th."

I kept my hunting in America after that. I never knew I crossed the border. Snowshoe hare are good in tourtière. You can use any combo of meats. Oh, and I have made it with all rabbit too. Don't tell my wife's relatives, but it is good with just one kind of ground meat too.

Ingredients: 1 pound of venison, 1 pound of rabbit meat, 1-2 onions, olive oil, ¾ cup of broth (your choice) 1 cup mashed potatoes, garlic powder, black pepper, and pie crust (homemade or store bought).

1. Grind 1 lb. of venison and 1 lb. of rabbit/hare.
2. Chop one large onion. Okay, maybe two onions, if you want.
3. Cook the onions in a frying pan with olive oil until soft.
4. Mix the rabbit and venison together with your hands while onions are cooking.
5. Add the meat to the onions and cook until it is brown.
6. Add 3/4 cup of broth and 1 cup of mashed potatoes (it binds the whole thing together).
7. Add garlic powder and black pepper (use 1-2 tablespoons of each. You know what you like).
8. Simmer until most liquid is absorbed.
9. Chill the meat for a couple of hours.
10. Use store-bought crust or your homemade. Put bottom pie crust in your 9" pie plate.
11. Remove the pie filling from the fridge and pat firm into the pan.
12. Add top crust. Do that whole egg wash thing to the top crust and cut some ventilation slits.
13. Bake at 375 degrees for 45 minutes or until golden brown.

Pasta with Meat Sauce

I grew up in a German-American home. I ate potatoes every day of my life, it seemed. I've had them raw-fried, boiled and fried, mashed, baked, leftover mashed spuds cooked as potato pancakes, scalloped, twice baked, and probably some ways that I cannot remember. Every day we had them, sometimes for two meals per day. Then there was meat and a vegetable. The starch, however, was always taters. It got to be that I was just not interested in eating them. When I left home at 18 years old, I never voluntarily consumed another "apple of the earth" as the French call them, until I was over 30 years old. If a restaurant selection came with a choice of potato, I would beg for anything else.

"I will take raw kale that is about to go bad, if I can substitute for the potato," I once said.

I loved Italian food as a kid and still do. My dad wouldn't touch the stuff, as he wasn't fond of any pasta. Occasionally he would eat pizza. He also refused to eat rice, because his service during WWII was in the Philippine Islands as a Sea Bee, and he ate rice with every single meal. Getting Italian food wasn't easy, though my mom would make spaghetti for my sister and me sometimes if dad was working and not home for supper.

One time, in school, I was asked, "You like that cafeteria spaghetti?"

"Yeah," I answered,"

"I'm Italian," he said, "And I can tell you that this stuff is nasty."

"I even eat the Chef Boyardee stuff in the cans," I said. He looked at me like I had just confessed to cannibalism.

The first time I got to eat pasta in an Italian home I was just amazed. I once was hunting on state game lands and met an elderly hunter who was hunting rabbits without a dog. He asked if he could hunt with me, and I said that he could, but we could not shoot the rabbits when we first saw them, the dogs had to chase the bunny in at least one circle because it was dangerous to shoot while the rabbit was close to the dogs. Once the rabbit ran for a circle, it would be a safe distance from the dogs. I shot my limit, he got one.

"I was hoping to get enough rabbit meat for my wife to make spaghetti sauce," he said.

"Yeah?" I asked.

"She makes a fantastic meat sauce with rabbit. She does it different than her mom did in the old country. She takes out the bones because she is always careful to remove the pellets. Her mom used tame rabbits that were not shot. Her mom grew up in Sicily. My wife just takes out the bones at the same time."

"Interesting," I said.

"And she cheats a little by using garlic paste at the end. And she uses a crockpot to make it at night," he said. I was intrigued.

"If you call your wife and get the recipe," I said, "I will trade you my four rabbits for it," I pulled the bunnies out of my vest. He pulled an old flip phone out of his pocket.

Ingredients: 4-6 rabbits, 1-2 onions, 2-4 peppers of your choice, your favorite spaghetti sauce, oregano, basil, and garlic paste.

1. Start this dish after supper, or before bed in your slow cooker.
2. Chop one onion, a couple of peppers of your choice, and a few mushrooms. Dice them all as small as you can and throw them in your slow cooker.
3. Add enough rabbit meat (no bones) to fill the crockpot a little over halfway.
4. Add enough of your favorite spaghetti sauce (you know what you like) to fill the slow cooker to 2/3 or 3/4 full.
5. Set the slow cooker on the setting that will bring your crockpot to a slow boil. I let it cook overnight. By morning the meat is thoroughly cooked. You can then set the slow cooker to the lowest setting to keep it warm or you can let it cook. The longer it cooks the more robust the tomato flavor and the more finely shredded the meat becomes. I have used venison roast instead of rabbit and cooked the sauce for 20 hours before.
6. I add oregano, garlic paste, and basil during the last hour of cooking. It stands out a little better than when it is cooked the entire time. Especially the garlic.
7. Spoon the sauce over your pasta shape of choice!

Rabbit Cacciatore

Cacciatore, means "in the style of the hunter" and almost any meat can be cooked in this style. Typically, it is a one-pan method. I presume this is because the hunter carries the pan into the woods, and decides to eat right after hunting, using a few vegetables that are brought along. I can tell you that this is one recipe that I have cooked in the field after shooting my limit, and just let the dogs chase a few more rabbits while I cooked.

When I think of hunting, I am prompted to think of rabbit hunting partners that I have had in my life. One was Roger Alderman, and some may recognize the name because he was heavily involved in the old SPO magazine that once catered to small pack option beagle field trials. Towards the end of his life, he wasn't hunting much and mostly ran his dogs inside the Corning Beagle Club. I was a member there when they got their first check from the company that found natural gas in the shale. The check was over ½ million dollars, as I recall. They promptly replaced the old 4'foot mesh fence with a 6' chain-link version. You would rarely see a deer.

Roger still went to field trials and a dog that was spayed or neutered could not compete then. He had a dog that needed to be spayed for medical reasons at a relatively young age, and he asked me to find a kid that wanted to hunt. I knew this dog could really chase a rabbit and got the dog to give to a kid at church.

As good as the dog was at chasing rabbits, she could not resist the temptations of deer. She had never run outside the chain-link fence and was therefore never taught to NOT chase them. The dog never did make it as a hunting dog. She once was found 12 miles away, in a garage. The owner of the garage had the upstairs of the building devoted to fly fishing, and it had all the tools and material necessary for making flies. The beagle got up there and curled up on an old deer hide that the fly fisherman was using to make his dry flies. Of course, it was a deer hide.

That being said, Roger was a devoted hunter in his youth. He once, even late in life, took me to a favorite spot of his that was located adjacent to a golf course. The rabbits were abundant and the chases were furious. The dogs were having a blast. I remember missing a few rabbits early on. Then I connected with one. Roger did some missing too, and he got one. Soon we each had 3 rabbits in the vest, but our percentage of hits was a little low. All the noise brought a golf course employee to see me. Keep in mind, this was in the winter, and we were not on the course itself.

"What are you doing?!" the man yelled.

"I am hunting rabbits," I said.

"Who told you that you could do that?"

"Roger Alderman," I said. The employee had never heard of Roger, so I introduced the two men.

"Who told you that you could hunt here?" the guy said.

"I don't remember his name," Roger answered, "That was more than 20 years ago!" We were done hunting there. Cacciatore.

Ingredients: Hind legs from 4 rabbits, 1 large onion, 3 stalks of celery, 5-6 carrots, eggs, flower, 7 cloves of garlic, 1 cup of mushrooms, 1 can stewed tomatoes, 1 box carton broth, oregano, thyme, sage, basil, rosemary, fresh olives, capers (optional), and pasta or rice.

1. Finely cut the following vegetables into a pile: a BIG onion, 5 or 6 sweet banana peppers, 3 stalks of celery, 5 or 6 carrots. Set these aside.
2. Take 8 hind legs of rabbit, dredge them in egg and flour. Fry them in the BIG and DEEP skillet until golden brown on both sides, and then remove from the skillet.
3. Put the finely chopped vegetables in the skillet and cook them until soft.
4. Add 7 cloves of garlic, chopped fine.
5. Add a cup of mushrooms. I like wild mushrooms, but if you cannot get these safely use store-bought. I often use 2 cups of mushrooms.
6. When the vegetables and mushrooms are cooked soft, add a splash of wine or balsamic vinegar to get the tasty crust off the bottom of the skillet.
7. Add a can of stewed tomatoes, and a can of chicken broth.
8. Add a thin dusting (a bit more than a teaspoon) of the following: oregano, thyme, sage, basil, and rosemary.
9. Add a couple of handfuls of olives and a small jar of capers.
10. Put the browned rabbit legs back on top, cover with a lid, and let simmer until the meat falls off the bone.
11. Serve over pasta or rice if so inclined.

Rabbit in a Hole

One of the realities of hunting rabbits is that they are a prey species for just about everything that eats meat. Hawks, Owls, fox, coyotes, weasel, fisher, mink, bobcat, feral house cat, snakes, and anything else you can mention. Crows will kill the babies in their nest. We have lots of competition. Those of us that hunt rabbits know that they tend to go into groundhog holes, just because of all the predators.

One of the dangerous things that some hunters will do is shoot at a rabbit, the moment that the dogs flush it from its hiding spot. Oftentimes, a dog is very close to the rabbit when it first begins to chase, and shooting while there is such a close distance between the dogs and the rabbit has a lot of risk—you could shoot the dog. I do not do it, and I will not let people that hunt with me shoot rabbits on the jump. All rabbits get to run one circle, at least. After the rabbit runs out and plays tricks, it will be further ahead of the dogs, providing a safe shot.

I understand why guys do this because oftentimes the rabbit will run straight to a hole. It might run 100 yards in a straight line, and go underground. I have places where I hunt that I can almost predict when it will happen, just by the way a chase starts. I like to hunt those places in the rain because I think a wet rabbit tends to stay above ground. It seems like rabbits tend to get into a groundhog hole before the rain and stay there until the weather has passed. I find that it is harder to find a rabbit in the rain because they have gone subterranean before the drizzle started; but the rabbits that remained above ground tend to stay above ground, usually.

Regardless, I think letting those rabbits go underground is what preserves a good hunting population for the next year. The quicker the rabbits go to ground in a given place, the more evidence I tend to see of predators. The critters I mentioned above live on bunnies all year long. At the parish I serve, there was a church member named Dutch when I first moved there. He hunted all the time, and when he was retired he could outwalk a lot of young guys in the woods. He was AAA, anti-aircraft artillery, in WWII and his hearing was not good. His vision was spot on, and he could shoot with the best of them. When he was younger, he owned beagles.

I had not been at the parish long before everyone realized I had beagles. In my second year, Dutch had mentioned that he would like to rabbit hunt. He had trouble hearing dogs like he had trouble hearing everything. Ears are how you can tell when the rabbit is beginning to circle back—the dogs start getting louder. They always circle, but they aren't perfect circles, and they can intersect at one point, and then on a fourth or fifth circle the bunny might move out a bit and start circling there. Hearing is a major asset in determining when the dogs were getting closer, and what angle they might come past where you are waiting in ambush. Even with perfect hearing, you can fail to get a glimpse of the wily prey, as it dodges you on the way to thick cover or a groundhog hole.

"Dutch," I said aloud, "I got a spot 200 yards from where I jump rabbits. Every rabbit I jump goes to this big dirt mound. The mound is covered with woodchuck holes. If I keep track of the dogs, will you shoot a few for me?"

"Yeah," he said, and that is just what we did. It wasn't a bunch of long chases, but it was a good time for a retired houndsman to shoot some rabbits and hear the chase, even if he had trouble determining where the dogs were, exactly. It violated my one circle rule, but the shooting was safe, because the rabbits were flushed in thick cover, and they stayed well behind the rabbit. The mound was small enough that in standing on the top of it, he could see the rabbits coming, no matter what approach they utilized. Dutch passed away, but that is one of my fondest hunts.

I call this recipe Rabbit in the Hole. When you cut them in half, you can see the ground pepper and the cooked rabbit inside.

Ingredients: 1-2 rabbits, 5-6 peppers, bag of shredded cheese, and 2 cans of crescent rolls.

1. Cook ground rabbit with hot peppers (whatever kind you like) in a frying pan and let cool. You must precook the meat, as it will not be cooked thoroughly from the time in the oven.
2. Take peppers (Hungarian wax, sweet banana, habanero—whatever you want) and remove the stem end.
3. Scoop out the seeds and membranes from the peppers.
4. Microwave the peppers on high for about a minute—just to get them flexible.
5. Put a little cheddar cheese in the bottom of the hollow pepper, pack it full of ground rabbit (or near full) and then put a little more shredded cheddar on top to fill the pepper to the brim!
6. Wrap the stuffed peppers in crescent rolls. It may take several of the rolls to cover each pepper. You can flatten the crescent dough to make it stretch further, or leave it thicker. Cover the entire pepper.
7. Bake until the rolls are brown. It will take longer than the crescent roll directions indicate.

This recipe works with ground venison, or whatever other meat you want to use.

Rabbit Scampi

Laura Sifford lived to be over 100 years old. She was a church member of mine, and she lived on her own until after she turned 100. Then, she had to go into a nursing home, and this particular home was a residence that had been converted into housing for a few senior citizens. You have probably seen the kind of place, the staff isn't well-paid, and they are always looking to save costs. Let's just say that the meals are often geared to toddlers more than retirees. I was at one of these small places at mealtime when the old-timers were fed macaroni and cheese with hotdogs—like it was summer camp for kindergarteners.

I went rabbit hunting in the morning one Saturday and managed to shoot my limit. The dogs were really enthused, and I gave them a drink of water and put them into the dog box in my truck, while I had an apple and a sandwich for lunch. The day was still young, and I took off my coveralls. I was wearing a pair of old Dockers underneath, and a T-shirt. I rooted around the back seat of my truck and found a button-down "brush shirt" that looked like it was nice enough for doing a visit. Some church members would be fine with coveralls, but in other instances I need to be a bit more formal. I swapped my boots for a pair of deck shoes that stay in the truck for instances like this, and I went to see Laura.

"Laura is not in her room," I said, fearing the worst. After all, she was 100 years old.

"She likes to go to the senior center for lunch," a gal in the kitchen said. She was chain-smoking cigarettes by an open window, in a building where half the residents were on oxygen.

"Oh yeah?" I asked.

"Yep, she doesn't like our food," another woman said, as she was cleaning up what looked like tater tots from the lunch that had just been served, "She will be back soon. The van will drop her off." Just then, the door slowly opened, and in walked Laura, taking slow steps with her walker, methodically moving the walker a few inches forward, and taking a small step. Then, moving the walker a few more inches forward, and taking another step. She had something resting on the walker. It was long enough that it could span the entire width of the handles, with significant overhang on each side.

"Hi Laura!" I said.

"I'll be right there, Pastor," she inched along. After what seemed like 100 tiny steps, she paused at the kitchen and handed the item on her walker to the chain smoker. "Here," Laura said, "This is some garlic bread that I got from the senior center. Some people might like a piece with their spaghetti. God knows you serve it often enough here. Come on, Pastor, we will visit in the living room." She inched her way in tiny steps towards a sofa.

I cooked scampi with the rabbits for supper that night, and I always serve my rabbit scampi over spaghetti noodles. I guess the events at the nursing home helped me to decide what to cook. Ever since that day, I serve garlic bread with the scampi too. As I ate my supper, I thought about that encounter between Laura and the staff. She had clearly noticed that they were saving money as best they could by serving spaghetti very frequently. Her mind stayed sharp until the end. She did not quite make 101.

Ingredients: 2-4 rabbits, egg wash with flour, 2 onions, 2 bulbs of garlic, butter, olive oil, broth (your choice), pasta shape you have on hand, and parmesan cheese.

1. Butcher 2-4 rabbits (four legs and miniature "back straps" for each).
2. Parboil rabbit pieces for 30 minutes.
3. Drain rabbit and dip each piece into egg and then flour.
4. Chop 2 onions and dice small. Sautee them in butter until brown.
5. Take 2 bulbs of garlic and separates into peeled cloves.
6. Add garlic to pan with onions, it can overcook fast. Cook until garlic is golden.
7. In pan melt a stick of butter with 1/4 cup olive oil and 1/4 cup broth.
8. Add black pepper to the butter and oil. If you like hot pepper flakes add some.
9. Combine the garlic and onion with the sauce and let simmer on low.
10. Start boiling spaghetti, or linguini, or angel hair pasta.
11. Fry the rabbits in the pan you cooked the onions and garlic.
12. Drain pasta and add it to the scampi sauce (which is with the garlic and onions).
13. Add copious quantities of parmesan cheese to the pasta and mix well.
14. Serve browned rabbit over the pasta.

Rabboli

When I go to field trials with my dogs, I often arrive the night before. I make pizzas in a propane oven, at high temperatures 400 degrees or hotter. I use tortillas, instead of pizza dough or crust. In large part, I do this because it is way easier to transport a pack of flour tortilla shells. Toppings, of course, can be whatever you want. They are a huge hit with my fellow competitors, and there have been times when people brought cheese to the trials, hoping I would be there. Inevitably, that is the ingredient that runs out first.

Now, if I am eating at a place that specializes in pizzas, I often prefer the Stromboli. I am not sure why this is the case, because it is basically the same ingredients. One time, my wife and I were at home and she asked if I could make a road-friendly Stromboli, one that could be done from a camping setup with just propane or charcoal available. I decided to test it at home.

"What is that?" she asked me.

"What does it look like?"

"A really weird pizza," she said.

"It is my camping Stromboli," I said.

"Get out of here!"

"I sliced it into pieces, separate them."

"Wait, what is this?" she looked at the layer of toppings inside, and the layer of toppings on top.

"Well," I said, "I walked around the bread aisle."

"Okay," she took a bite.

"And I stopped at the pitas."

"A pita?"

"Or …" I said, "A really thin crust Stromboli, but better since there are toppings on top. And inside. Stromboli has all the toppings inside."

"Is it a taco Stromboli?"

"Umm. Yeah. This one is.

"Why the pita?"

"It is easy to transport, like tortilla shells. And, they are small enough to do in a camping scenario."

That being said, it also is a hit at home, especially in the winter when we will run the oven, and invite some friends over. They can be made with any toppings, but my favorite is with ground rabbit as the meat inside.

Ingredients: Gyro pitas, Taco seasoning, pizza sauce, pesto, garlic paste, fresh mozzarella, shredded parmesan, and pepperoni.

1. I make burger out of rabbits, deboning them and then putting the meaty though the KitchenAid grinder.
2. I fry the ground rabbit in a pan with a little olive oil, since it is so lean.
3. This next step is so easy and plain that I am almost embarrassed to admit it. I season the meat with a McCormick spice from the store that is literal labelled "Taco." That is it. I have also seasoned the burger with red pepper flakes and onion powder instead of the "Taco" seasoning.
4. Slice the pita open, but do not fully separate it.
5. I mix pizza sauce, pesto, and garlic paste to make my base layer inside the pita. I use roughly equal amounts of each, but that may be too much garlic for some people.
6. That inside layer of sauce then gets topped with the seasoned rabbit burger and tiny bits of fresh mozzarella.
7. I close the pita and use pizza sauce for the top of the pita. I typically use the shredded parmesan cheese on the top layer, and then pepperoni. Not the powdered parmesan, the sliced.
8. Bake at 400 degrees. It won't take long, but keep your eye on them, as you will be making more than one. The rabbit is already cooked, so when the cheese is melted, it is done. Cooking time increases as you lose heat opening the door and making more, especially while camping. But it is just a few minutes typically.
9. I slice it into 4 pieces, and enjoy the reaction. Most people will think that it is a single layer pizza, with cheese and pepperoni, until they take that first bite and get the rabbit, garlic, pesto, and fresh mozzarella on the inside.
10. By all means, experiment with toppings. I like caramelized onions, artichokes, olives, and finely minced banana peppers the best, but the sky is the limit.

40-Clove Rabbit

Sometimes, a recipe comes to mind just out of happenstance. I was rabbit hunting with a friend of mine, and he said that he would pack the lunch. It was a Saturday and we planned on hunting all day.

"I brought coffee," I said to Lee when I picked him up to go hunting.

"You can keep that," he said, "I would drink it if it tasted as good as it smelled."

We headed to the spot we were hunting and within a few minutes, we had a rabbit running fast and furious, making loops in the goldenrod, and then dashing across an open area to make circle in the pines. That small opening between the goldenrod and the pines provided the only shooting. We took turns shooting rabbits, and by lunch we had managed to get three rabbits. We took the dogs back to the truck to give them a drink of water, and we broke out lunch. Lee had bottled water, and I produced a thermos of coffee. "You sure?" I offered him a cup.

"No thank you," he said as he opened a small cooler.

"What did you bring?"

"Italian hoagies," he said.

"Sounds good to me."

Each one was about a foot long, with ham, bologna, and salami. I took a bite. "Man, this is good," I said.

"I think it will be fine," Lee took a bit.

"What kind of roll is this?" I asked.

"Well," Lee paused as he often does when he is about to explain something a bit out of the ordinary, "When I woke up this morning the kids had left us out of rolls and bread."

"This looks like bread," I said.

"Well, yeah," Lee said, "So, I got into the freezer and we had one of those frozen loaves of garlic bread in there. I baked it, cut it in half, and made two hoagies."

"I'm pretty impressed."

We finished lunch, moved to a new hunting spot, and by three o'clock in the afternoon, we had both shot our limit of rabbits. I dropped him off and went home.

"I am home," I kissed Renee.

"Whew," she said, "You were eating garlic."

"Yeah, at lunch," I said.

"They say that if a couple eats garlic together, they won't smell each other. I got four rabbits, know anything that we can make that uses lots of garlic?"

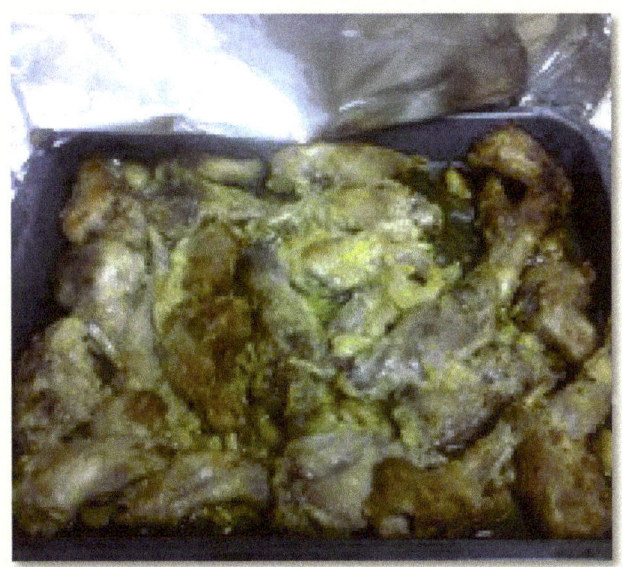

You have heard of 40-clove chicken? Try it with rabbit! Mix all this in the same pan and put it in the oven at 350 for 90 minutes or so—until the bunny is cooked, but not dry.

Ingredients: 3-4 rabbits, 40 cloves of garlic, 2 onions, 1-2 cups of mushrooms, black pepper, paprika, chicken stock, and olive oil.

1. 3-4 rabbits cut into pieces. Place on a large sheet so the meat is one layer.
2. 2 onions, chopped small.
3. 1-2 cups of the mushrooms of your choice cut fine—I like wild mushrooms.
4. Black pepper.
5. A shake of paprika to put a light coating on each piece of rabbit.
6. 40 cloves of peeled garlic—I just use a couple of bulbs, however many cloves it is.
7. Enough chicken stock to cover the bottom of the pan.
8. A bit of olive oil on top of the rabbit to brown it in the oven.

Spicy Sauerkraut and Rabbit

Have you ever had to live on your own for a week or two? My wife, Renee, is frequently away for work. Granted, these are work conferences, but all the pictures that she sends me are in restaurants and shopping centers. Or beaches. These conferences never take place in Cleveland during January. Or even Cleveland in the summer. It tends to be Florida, California, or Vegas. Oftentimes, they are at the peak of winter too. Off she goes to Orlando, works the day away, and then hits Disney. I will end up cooking for myself in Pennsylvania.

Winter is also hunting season, and that means that I will be in the woods pursuing more rabbits. I will usually eat the same dish every night while she is gone. It is called *szegediner krautfleisch*, and I first had it at an Austrian restaurant. It is basically spicy sauerkraut, with meat cooked in with the sauerkraut. It is perfect because my wife is not a fan of spicy foods. I mean, she likes a standard Buffalo wing, but nothing too hot. I can get my fill of this favorite dish, knowing that it would be too hot for her.

So, before I leave to go hunting for the first day of her trip, I put all the ingredients into the slow cooker. When I return that evening, the dish is ready, I then put the leftovers in the refrigerator, and I will heat some up every night. I may have it with mashed potatoes one night, home fries another, and maybe pierogies if I have any in the freezer. The dish is traditionally made with pork, but I use rabbits. When the winter nights bring fresh blankets snow, it really helps me to see the cottontails, and my game vest gets more use. This is a dish that warms me up on a cold evening.

"Hello?" I answered a call from my wife, who was in Orlando.

"I just called to say hello. Long day at the conference."

"Glad you are doing well. Where are you now?"

"Just left the hotel to go out for supper."

"I miss you!"

"I miss you too," I said.

"What have you been up to?"

"Just eating leftovers."

"We will have to fix that when I get home."

"Sounds good to me," I said.

"Okay, well, we are getting out of the Uber to eat now."

"Okay, have fun."

"Love you."

"You too."

Hey, I hunt until dark every day that she is away. That can get me in trouble when she is home. And *szegediner krautfleisch* is one dish that I think gets better when you reheat it.

Combine the following in a crockpot and cook for 10 hours or so...

Ingredients: 3-4 rabbits, can of beer or 12 ounces of apple cider, paprika, black pepper, hot pepper flakes, 1 onion, and minced garlic or garlic paste.

1. 2 bags of sauerkraut (2 lbs. each).
2. De-boned meat of 3-4 rabbits.
3. Can of beer or some apple cider.
4. A tablespoon of Paprika.
5. A tablespoon of black pepper.
6. Crushed red pepper—I like it hot, you decide.
7. A few shakes of Old Bay seasoning,
8. One diced onion.
9. For the last hour, I squirt in some Garlic paste or minced garlic. About a tablespoon is good for me, and make sure you don't overcook the stuff, or it will get bitter.

Conclusion

My wife is more sophisticated than I am. Granted, this is as obvious as a horsefly on a powdered donut hole to anyone that knows me. You see, my wife, Renee, travels a lot for her work at the university. She has been to Disney more than all my relatives combined because that is where academic conferences tend to occur. Well, she has also been to Vegas more than a career gambler too. Sin City is another popular destination for her work conferences. She is also a big fan of trying new things at our local restaurants too.

"Why don't you try the smoked pig cheeks?" she asked me one time.

"Because," I said, "I don't know if I will like it. I know I like brisket, so I got that."

"Well," she dismissed my hesitance, "You were probably a picky eater as a kid too. Did you always choose the same thing then?"

"Yeah," I said, "I chose what my mother cooked. The other option was to not eat at all."

That, I suppose, is why I tend to not order things I have never tried while at a restaurant. Going without food as a kid was free. Going without food at a restaurant costs $20 plus tip. Incidentally, I tried pork cheek at a pig roast not long ago, and it was delicious. One night this summer, I trained the hunting beagles until dark and then went home. I fed the dogs, put my Tek 2.0 SportDOG tracking collars on the charging station, and poured a big glass of iced tea.

"What do you want for supper?" Renee asked.

"I am flexible," I said, "It is hot outside, so I am not in the mood to eat much. Maybe another glass of tea will be enough. Something cold."

"How about charcuterie?" she asked.

"What?"

"You like it. Remember, you had it when we were at the restaurant last month."

"I doubt it," I said.

"It was served on a wooden board. There was salami, capicola, brie, feta, and cheddar," Renee counted each item on her fingers as she looked to the ceiling to jar her memory.

"Oh. Well, yeah, why don't you just call it processed meat and cheese."

"Preserved. Not processed. Charcuterie is a variety of processes to preserve meat, and it is intended for you to savor the flavors that are bestowed by curing and smoking."

"Um. Okay. I will eat breadless sandwiches if that is what you are in the mood for," I said, "It can be on a regular plate too if we don't have any extra cutting boards laying around."

On another instance, Renee called me when she was on her way to a meeting, "Can you make tapas for us tonight?" she asked.

"If you tell me where to find one," I said.

"No!" she said, "Don't you remember we had tapas together?"

"You mean that tilapia fish?"

"I mean tapas. Small plates meant to be shared."

"Small plates of what?"

"Well," Renee sighed, "It can be whatever you want. We have some chicken leftovers, and some pasta salad, and a few hard-boiled eggs that could be deviled."

"Oh," I said, "Yeah. I can cook some warm-ups."

"What are warm-ups?"

"You sophisticated people call it leftovers."

"Well, yes. Our tapas will be leftovers, but that is not what it means. It is small plates of food intended to be shared."

"So, you mean appetizers?"

"Whatever, can you make it? I will be home at eight o'clock tonight."

"And your warm-up appetizers will be waiting!" I said. She just hung up.

At the beginning of August, I was getting the freezer ready for the upcoming hunting season. I had a couple of rabbits in there, a bit of venison, one pheasant, a grouse, and two doves.

"I am bringing home some company" a text from my wife appeared on my phone. I was running dogs. I ignored the text.

"Can you get supper for everyone?" she texted again.

"I guess," I typed back.

"Whatever you want to make is fine. Or buy something. Four people are coming."

"No problem."

"7 pm" she typed. I picked up the dogs and went home.

I made rabbit bratwurst, venison jerky, and noodle soup with all the gamebirds. I also made these peppers that I stuffed with ground venison that I cooked and then wrapped those same Hungarian wax peppers with crescent rolls. I baked them until they were done. The freezer was now ready for the fall hunting season.

"Wow," Renee said as she entered the house and smelled the food, "Where did you get delivery from?"

"I cooked," was my reply as I handed everyone a saucer. "This here meal is tapas, with a little bit of charcuterie in the form of venison jerky—perfectly preserved."

"What?" my wife looked nervous.

"I have rabbit bratwurst too, as well as some venison stuffed peppers and a chicken noodle soup made with pheasant, grouse, and dove instead of chicken."

"I have never tried rabbit," one guest said.

"Well," I replied, "It is free to you, which is the best way to try something new."

"This is good!" one guy said.

"Feel free to refill that little plate that goes with the coffee cup," I motioned towards the food, "My wife says that tapas are served on small plates."

"I like this bratwurst a lot," he answered, "Maybe you can teach me to hunt."

"Well, I suppose."

"What do I need?"

"Hmm," I said, "I can loan you a shotgun. Get a pair of brush pants, boots, a hunting vest, an orange hat, and take a hunter's safety course." Who would have thought that these sophisticated types would become hunters because of the desire to try new food? Supper tables are the future for converting people to our sport. Well, my wife calls it dinner, but you know what I mean. It is supper.

For more, go to www.beaglebard.com

www.ingramcontent.com/pod-product-compliance
Lightning Source LLC
Chambersburg PA
CBHW061414090426
42742CB00023B/3464